Shape, Measures & Data Textbook

Peter Patilla
Ann Montague-Smith
Paul Broadbent

Addison Wesley Longman

Edinburgh Gate, Harlow, Essex, CM20, 2JE, England and
Associated Companies throughout the World

First published 1996

Designed and typeset by Gecko Design Limited
Illustrations by Gecko Ltd, Madeleine Baker, Phil Burrows,
Roger Fereday, Tania Hurt-Newton, Peter Richardson

Picture Researcher, Valerie Mulcahy; photo props collected
and made by Helen and Mark Mulcahy.

We are grateful to the following for permission to
reproduce photographs:

Gareth Boden, page 10, 21, 23, 29, 42, 43; Bruce Coleman
Limited, page 13 below right (Jeff Foott); Oxford Scientific
Films, pages 13 above right (Michael Fogden), 37 above left
(R L Manuel), 37 above right (Colin Milkins) 37 below
(Scott Camazine); Telegraph Colour Library/Planet Earth,
pages 13 above left (David A Ponton), 13 below left
(Tetrao Tetrix).

The publisher's policy is to use paper
manufactured from sustainable forests.

Printed in Hong Kong

We are grateful to the children and staff at Roger Ascham
Primary School for their invaluable help in creating the
photography for this book.

The publishers would also like to thank NES Arnold for
their co-operation and support in the making of this
scheme.

Shape, Measures & Data Textbook

CONTENTS

Shapes quiz

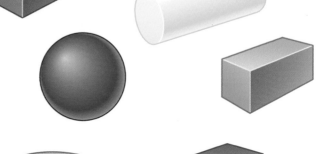

A What is my name?

1. I have 6 square faces.
   Who am I ?
2. I have 2 triangle faces and
   3 rectangle faces.
   Who am I ?
3. I have 2 square faces and
   4 rectangle faces. Who am I ?
4. I have 4 triangle faces.
   Who am I ?

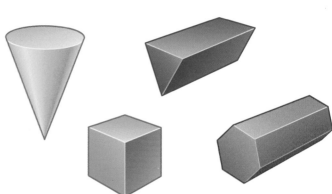

B Half and half
Here are halves of shapes.

1.
2.
3.
4.

Name the whole shapes.

C Posting shapes
A 3D shape will pass through the hole.
The shadow of the shape can be seen.
Name each shape.

1.
2.
3.
4.

D Shape names
Name each 4-sided shape.

1.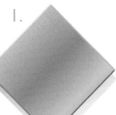
2.
3.
4.

E Symmetry
Write which of these shapes have a line of symmetry.

1.
   star
2.
   moon
3.
   cloud
4.
   sun

F Yes or No

Copy the table.
Draw each shape on the table.

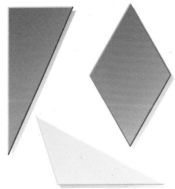

	Some right angles	No right angles
Some equal sides		
No equal sides		

Here is an arrow head.
It has also been drawn upside down.

A Copy each shape then draw it upside down.

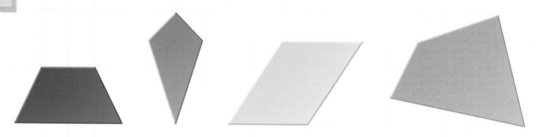

B Write which of these shapes are exactly the same as A.

This shape is reflected in a mirror.

mirror

A Copy each shape then draw the reflection.

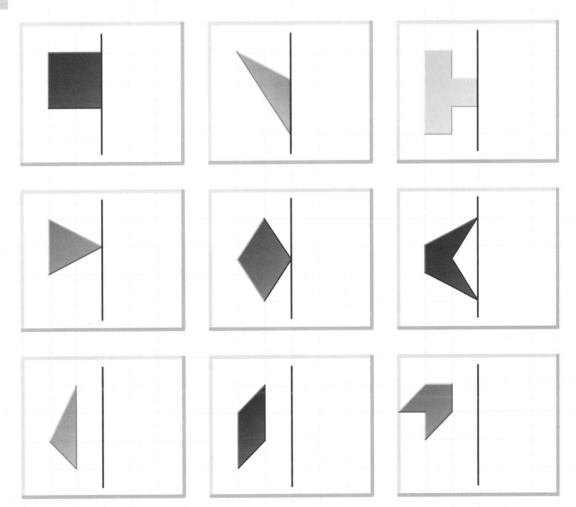

Shape patterns

A Choose an exploding shape pattern to make.

B Choose a starting shape.
Design an exploding pattern.

C 2D shapes can be arranged to leave gaps.
Which shapes have been used to leave these gaps?

1.
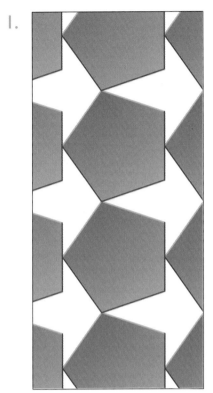

2.

3.
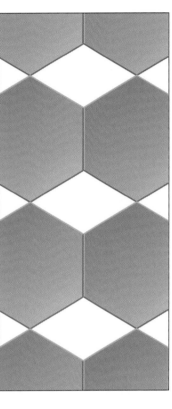

4.
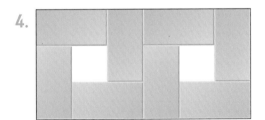

5.
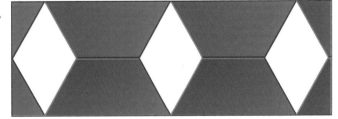

D Use 2D shapes.
Design your own pattern of gaps.

Circle patterns

Shape

Use a pair of compasses.
Draw and colour circle patterns.

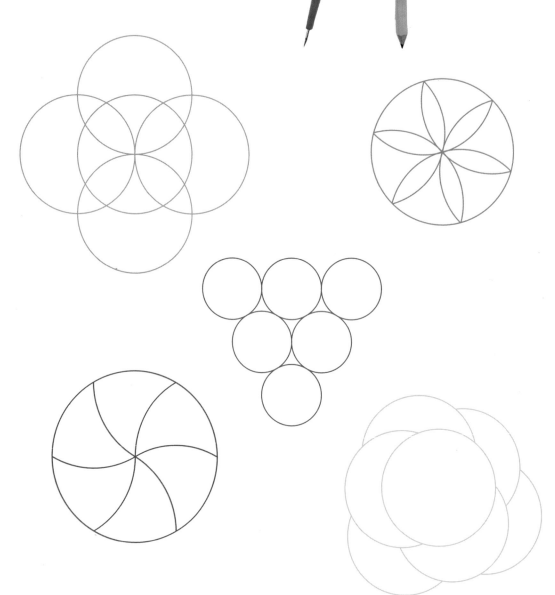

Challenge
Design your own circle pattern.

Shape

Border patterns

Use coloured marker pens.
Design some border patterns.

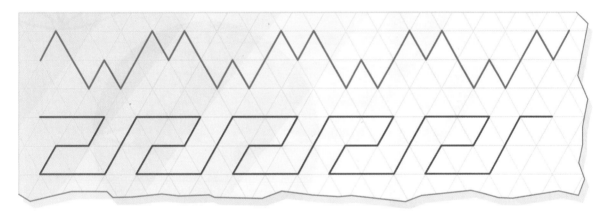

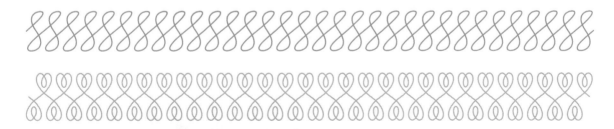

Challenge

Use Logo on a computer to
design a border pattern.

Rangoli patterns Shape

Did You Know ?

Decorating floors, walls
and steps for festive occasions
is a popular artistic tradition in India.
Rangoli floor patterns are well
known. In some parts of India they
are called Alpana.
Rangoli patterns are done freehand
inside a square, circle or rectangle.

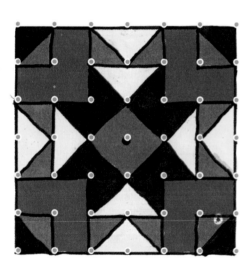

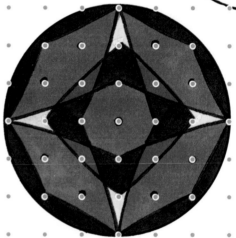

Challenge

Use spotty paper to
design your own
Rangoli patterns.

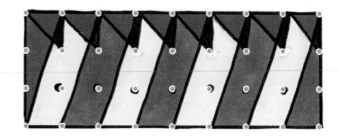

Nature patterns

Animals make patterns too.

Things to do

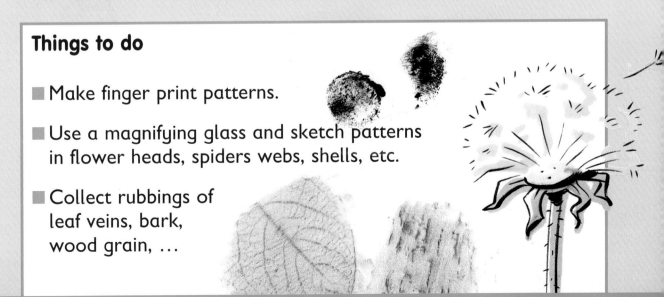

■ Make finger print patterns.

■ Use a magnifying glass and sketch patterns in flower heads, spiders webs, shells, etc.

■ Collect rubbings of leaf veins, bark, wood grain, ...

Logo stars

A Use Logo on a computer to draw a star.
Choose one of these or make your own.

I tried these …
REPEAT
TO or BUILD
SHOW and HIDE
PENUP and
PENDOWN

Challenge
Can you make your star
twinkle?

B Design a sky at night

I tried these …
PROCEDURES
Star
moon
church

SIZE
FILL

Logo: using REPEAT

Covering areas

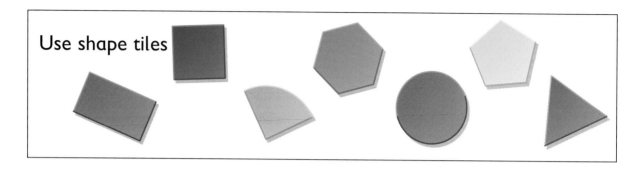

Use shape tiles

Approximately 12 rectangles cover this shape. The area of the shoe is about 12 rectangles.

A Draw round your shoe. Cover the drawing with shape tiles.

The area of my shoe is about

☐ rectangles

☐ squares

☐ triangles

☐ circles

B Use shape tiles to find the approximate area of these.

Tin lid   Hand   Book   String loop

C These two shapes have an area of 15 squares.

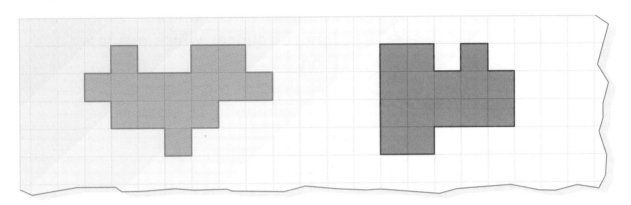

Use squared paper.
Draw two shapes each with an area of 15 squares.

D These two shapes have an
area of 15 triangles.

Use triangle paper.
Draw two shapes each with an area of 15 triangles.

INVESTIGATE

Draw a 3 × 3 square.

Cut along the red lines to make three pieces.
Investigate the different shapes you can make.

Finding areas

Count the whole squares.
Squares which are $\frac{1}{2}$ or more count as whole ones.
Ignore squares which are less than $\frac{1}{2}$.
The area of this shape is approximately 16 squares.

A Write the approximate areas of these shapes.

1.

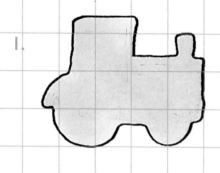

2.

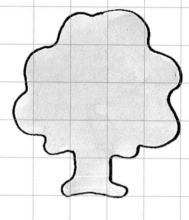

3.

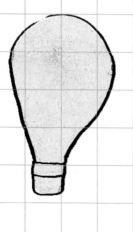

4.

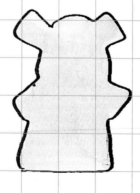

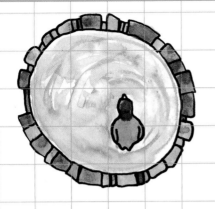
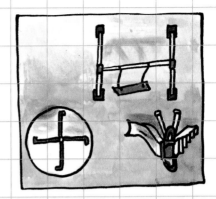
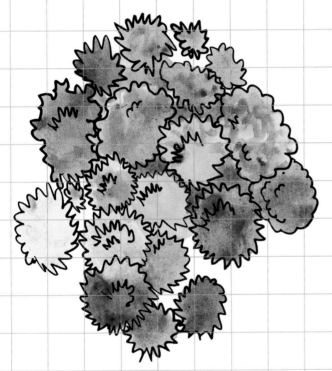
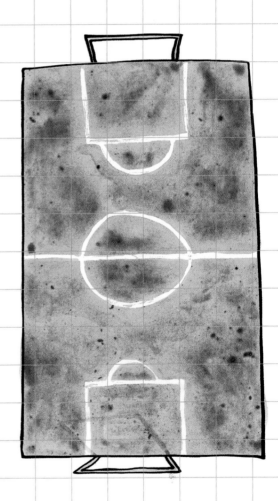

B Write the approximate areas of
1. pond
2. woodland
3. playground
4. football pitch

Long distances can be measured in kilometres.

> 1 kilometre = 1000 metres
>   1 km = 1000 m

A **10 km road race**

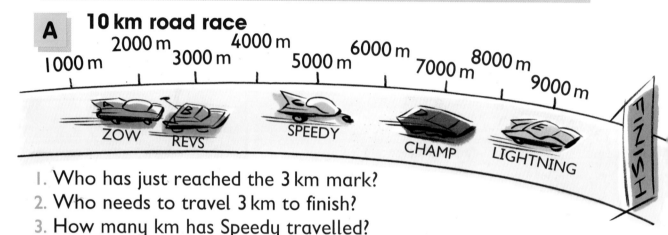

1. Who has just reached the 3 km mark?
2. Who needs to travel 3 km to finish?
3. How many km has Speedy travelled?
4. Who has travelled 6 km further than Revs?

B **Balloon race**

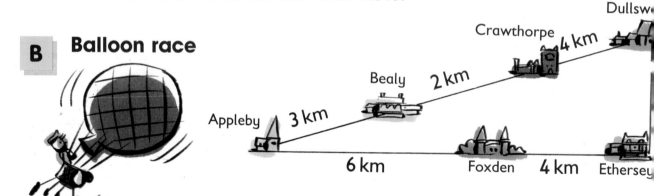

The balloon race starts from Appleby.
In which village did each balloon land?

1. Mighty Midge travelled 5000 metres.
2. Flighty Frank travelled 6000 metres.
3. Super Sid travelled 10 000 metres.
4. Daring Denis travelled 3000 metres.

Did You Know ?

Richard Branson travelled 4947 km in a hot air balloon in 31 hours 41 minutes.

Measures   ... and the short of it!

Short distances can be measured in millimetres.

10 millimetres = 1 centimetre
10 mm = 1 cm

A *Bungy jumping*
Measure these lines in millimetres.

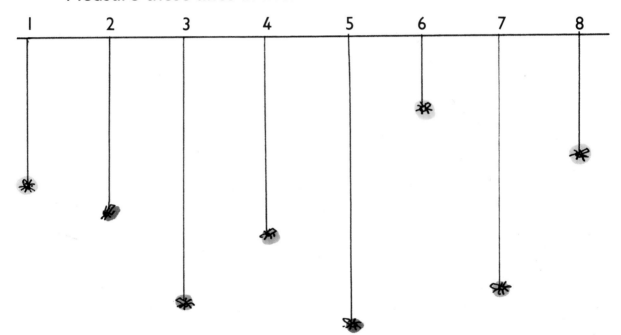

| 1 | 2 | 3 | 4 | 5 | 6 | 7 | 8 |

B *Leaf hopping*

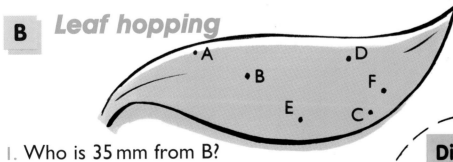

1. Who is 35 mm from B?
2. Who is 16 mm from A?
3. Who is 21 mm from D?
4. Who is 7 mm from F?

Did You Know ?

A flea can jump
about 180 mm high

Drawing challenge

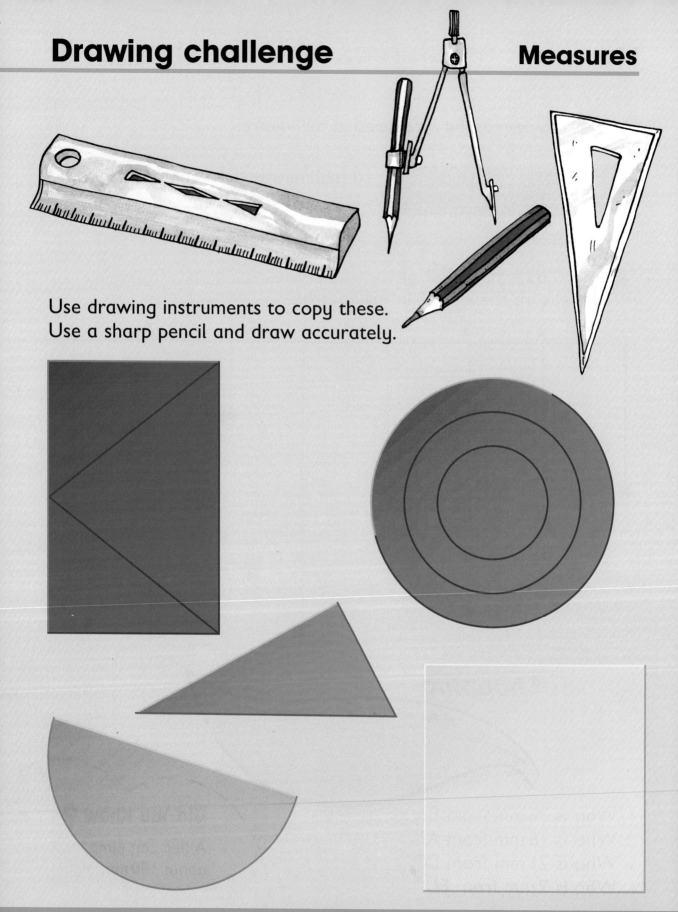

Use drawing instruments to copy these.
Use a sharp pencil and draw accurately.

Designer waistcoats

Design and make your own paper waistcoat.

Write the weight each shows.

A

1. KG
2. KG
3. KG
4. KG

B

1. KG
2. KG
3. KG
4. KG

C

grams | grams | grams | grams

1.
100
200
300
400

2.
100
200
300
400

3.
100
200
300
400
500
600
700
800

4.
100
200
300
400
500
600
700
800

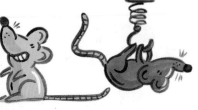
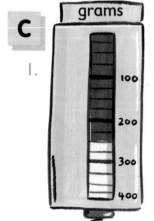
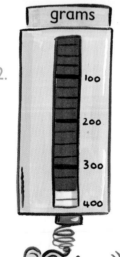

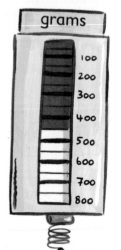

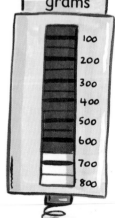

Measures

Sandwich survey

The pupils of Parks School are doing a food survey. They wondered what weight of sandwiches they ate in one week.

= 500 g

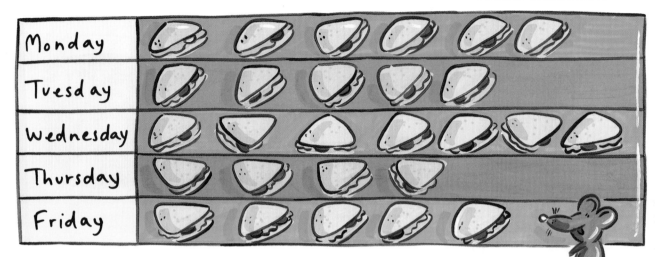

1. What weight of sandwiches was eaten on Tuesday?
2. On which day was 3500 g of sandwiches eaten?
3. What was the total weight of sandwiches eaten for the week?
4. Sandwiches weigh about 50 g. Approximately how many sandwiches were eaten during the week?
5. Carry out your own sandwich survey.

Challenge

Tom brings an apple every day for his teacher.

The apples weigh about 90 g each.

How many kilograms of apples does he bring the teachers in a year?

(Remember that school is closed for weekends and holidays.)

Weight: problem-solving

A How much more water is needed to make each of these 1 litre?

1.

2.

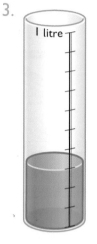

3.

4.

B Use containers which are marked to hold 1 litre.

 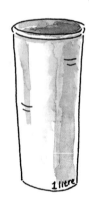 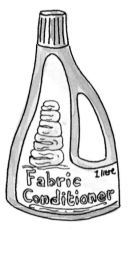 

When 1 litre is poured in there is still a space.
Estimate then check the true capacities
of the containers.

 Copy and complete the table.

Container	Total capacity		Capacity of space
	Estimate	Check	
Shampoo			

Water in the home

The Ross family kept a record of how much water they used in a day.

	Having a bath	Flushing toilets	Washing hands	Brushing teeth	Washing machine	Each drink	Having a shower	Washing up
Water used litres (l)	70 l	9 l	2 l	1 l	25 l	$\frac{1}{4}$ l	35 l	10 l
Number of times a day	1	15	20	10	1	14	2	3

A

1. How much water did they use for washing their hands?
2. Which activity used up most water?
3. Which activity used up least water?
4. Which used more water, using the washing machine or washing up?
5. Do they use more water each day having baths or showers?
6. How much water did the Ross family use altogether in one day?

B

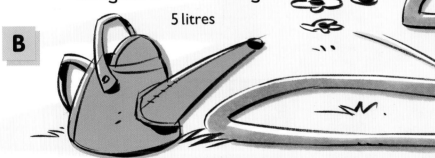

5 litres

7 litres each minute

Mr Ross hoses his garden for 15 minutes.
Mrs Ross uses the watering can.
How many times must Mrs Ross fill the watering can to use the same amount of water as Mr Ross?

Filling boxes

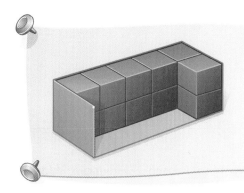

The box holds 2 layers of cubes.
It holds 10 cubes in the bottom layer.
It holds 20 cubes in total.
The volume of the box is 20 cubes.

A Put a layer of cubes in the bottom of a box.
Count the number of cubes.
Find how many layers are needed to fill the box.

 Record in a
table.
Repeat for
two different
boxes.

Box	Cubes in one layer	Number of layers	Volume in cubes
A			

B Use 24 cubes each time.
Build cuboids on these grids.
Record your results.

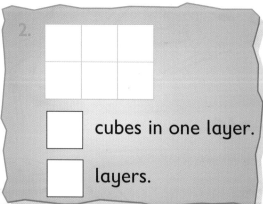

1.

☐ cubes in one layer.

☐ layers.

2.

☐ cubes in one layer.

☐ layers.

3.

☐ cubes in one layer.

☐ layers.

Measures   Tower blocks

A Build a city of tower blocks.
Each tower block must be different
and have a volume of 30 cubes.

B Draw these ground plans.
Write how many cubes are in each tower block.

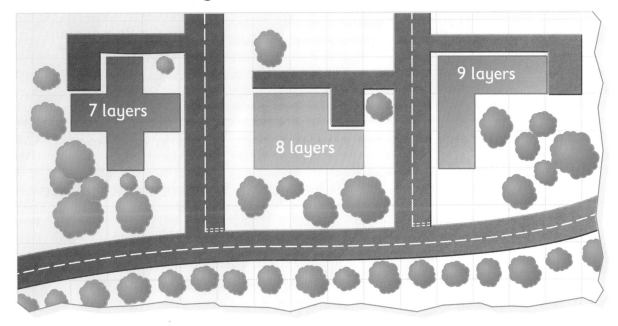

7 layers

8 layers

9 layers

Calendars

	JANUARY		FEBRUARY		MARCH		APRIL
M	4 11 18 25	M	1 8 15 22	M	1 8 15 22 29	M	5 12 19 26
T	5 12 19 26	T	2 9 16 23	T	2 9 16 23 30	T	6 13 20 27
W	6 13 20 27	W	3 10 17 24	W	3 10 17 24 31	W	7 14 21 28
T	7 14 21 28	T	4 11 18 25	T	4 11 18 25	T	1 8 15 22 29
F	1 8 15 22 29	F	5 12 19 26	F	5 12 19 26	F	2 9 16 23 30
S	2 9 16 23 30	S	6 13 20 27	S	6 13 20 27	S	3 10 17 24
S	3 10 17 24 31	S	7 14 21 28	S	7 14 21 28	S	4 11 18 25

	MAY		JUNE		JULY		AUGUST
M	3 10 17 24 31	M	7 14 21 28	M	5 12 19 26	M	2 9 16 23 30
T	4 11 18 25	T	1 8 15 22 29	T	6 13 20 27	T	3 10 17 24 31
W	5 12 19 26	W	2 9 16 23 30	W	7 14 21 28	W	4 11 18 25
T	6 13 20 27	T	3 10 17 24	T	1 8 15 22 29	T	5 12 19 26
F	7 14 21 28	F	4 11 18 25	F	2 9 16 23 30	F	6 13 20 27
S	1 8 15 22 29	S	5 12 19 26	S	3 10 17 24 31	S	7 14 21 28
S	2 9 16 23 30	S	6 13 20 27	S	4 11 18 25	S	1 8 15 22 29

	SEPTEMBER		OCTOBER		NOVEMBER		DECEMBER
M	6 13 20 27	M	4 11 18 25	M	1 8 15 22 29	M	6 13 20 27
T	7 14 21 28	T	5 12 19 26	T	2 9 16 23 30	T	7 14 21 28
W	1 8 15 22 29	W	6 13 20 27	W	3 10 17 24	W	1 8 15 22 29
T	2 9 16 23 30	T	7 14 21 28	T	4 11 18 25	T	2 9 16 23 30
F	3 10 17 24	F	1 8 15 22 29	F	5 12 19 26	F	3 10 17 24 31
S	4 11 18 25	S	2 9 16 23 30	S	6 13 20 27	S	4 11 18 25
S	5 12 19 26	S	3 10 17 24 31	S	7 14 21 28	S	5 12 19 26

A A Nature Watch Club meets on the second Tuesday in each month.
Write the dates of all the meetings.

B The club members cleared a canal bank. They started on May 15 and finished on July 7.
How many weekends did they work?

C The club goes to summer camp for a week beginning on the last Friday in July.
Write the holiday dates.

Did You Know ?

The first calendars were used by the Babylonians about 1800 BC.

This is a way to remember how many days are in each month.
Knuckle months

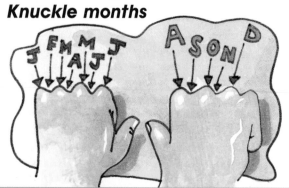

All the 'Knuckle months' have 31 days.
February has 28 days.
April, June, September and November have 30 days.

am and pm

am can be used to show morning times

8.20 in the morning
8.20 am

pm can be used to show afternoon or evening times

3.25 in the afternoon
3.25 pm

Saturday

Wake up call . Breakfast from am to .

Making a bird hide from to . Lunch from to .

Pond dipping from to . Supper from to

Campfire songs from to pm. Bed pm.

A
1. What time did the campfire start?
2. What time did breakfast end?
3. How long did lunch take?
4. Between lunch and pond dipping they went for a walk. How long did the walk take?
5. How long were they awake?

B Between pond dipping and supper two jobs must be done.
Which two would you choose?
How long would they take?

Jobs to do	
litter collecting	15 mins
peeling potatoes	30 mins
washing up	25 mins
collecting wood	30 mins
cooking supper	45 mins
making bird boxes	60 mins

Measuring angles

Measures

Angles are measured in degrees.
A right angle measures 90 degrees.

90°

A Choose shape tiles which have angles of 90°.
Draw round them and tick the 90° angles.

B Choose shape tiles which have angles smaller than 90°.
Draw round them and tick the angles smaller than 90°.

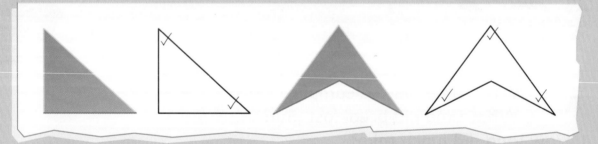

C Choose shape tiles which have angles larger than 90°.
Draw round them and tick the angles larger than 90°.

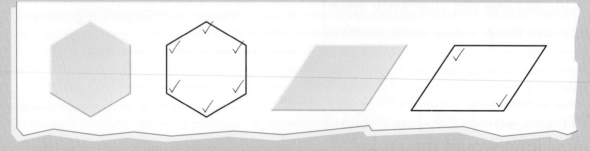

Measures Angle measurer

 A Make an angle measurer.

Trace the picture opposite
and cut it out.

Cut the thick line.

Cut out another circle.

Cut the thick line.

Slot the circles
together.

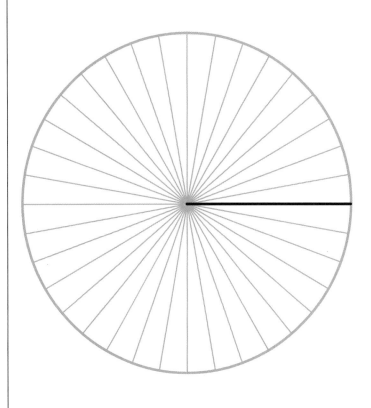

B Use your angle measurer to show angles of
10°   50°   80°   90°   120°   160°   300°

C Estimate these angle sizes.

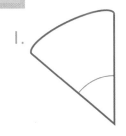 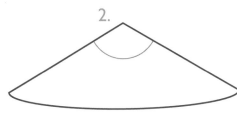 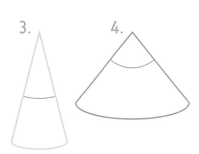

1.   2.   3.   4.

Using protractors

A protractor measures angles in degrees. This protractor measures each 10°.

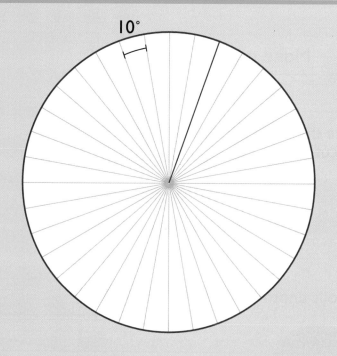

10°

A How many degrees do the shaded angles measure?

1.
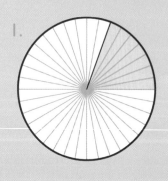

2.
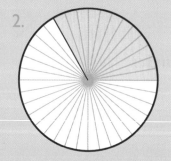

3.
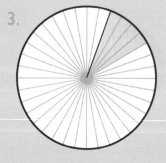

4.
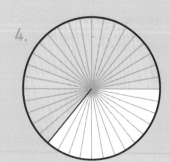

5.
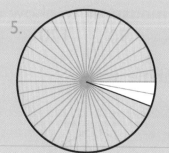

6.
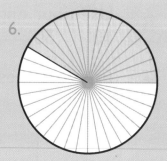

Measures

B Measure these angles to the nearest 10°.

1.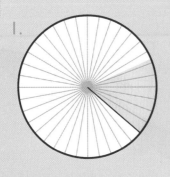
2.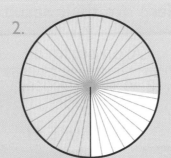
3.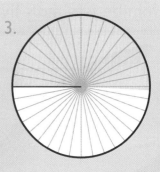

4.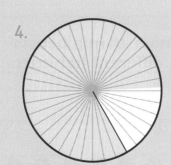
5.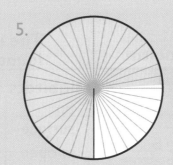
6.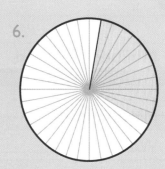

C Now measure these angles to the nearest 10°.

1.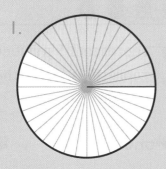
2.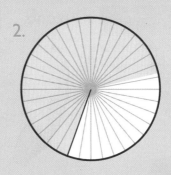
3.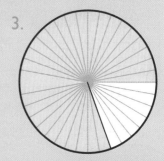

D Draw some angles.
Measure each one to the nearest 10°.

Pond dipping

Class 4 went pond dipping to find out where freshwater minibeasts may live. Here are their results.

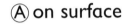

Ⓐ on surface   Ⓓ on plants

Ⓑ in open water

Ⓒ on pond bed

Minibeasts found	Habitat
Freshwater shrimp	B
Midge larvae	D
Water mites	B
Leeches	C
Pond skater	A
Water louse	C
Flat worm	C
Ramshorn snail	D
Water beetle	B

The number of minibeasts found in different habitats

habitats

on surface   🪲🪲

in open water   🪲🪲🪲🪲🪲🪲🪲🪲

on pond bed   🪲🪲🪲🪲

on plants   🪲🪲🪲🪲

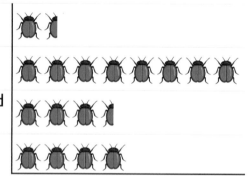

🪲 represents 5 minibeasts

🪲 represents fewer than 5 minibeasts

Pond dipping

Graph — Number of minibeasts found (y-axis, scale 2 to 28):

- Freshwater shrimp: 25
- Midge larvae: 18
- Water mites: 13
- Leeches: 9
- Pond skater: 6
- Water louse: 6
- Flat worm: 3
- Ramshorn snail: 2
- Water beetle: 2

A
1. Where were most minibeasts found?
2. How many leeches were found?
3. Which minibeasts were found on the pond bed?
4. How many minibeasts were found on plants?
5. How many more water mites than flat worms were found?
6. Which minibeast was most frequently found in open water?
7. How many minibeasts were found on the pond bed?
8. How many minibeasts were found altogether?

B These are part of a card database about freshwater minibeasts.

Freshwater shrimp	Ramshorn snail	Leech

Family: crustacean Length: 10 mm Body parts: many Habitat: open water	Family: mollusc Length: 12 mm Body parts: one Habitat: on plants and open water	Family: true worm Length: 15–40 mm Body parts: one Habitat: on pond bed

■ Continue this set of cards for other minibeasts. Use the information on these pages and other reference books.

■ Use a computer database to show this information.

Weather records

A London

1. Which date had the highest temperature?
2. What temperature was reached on the 4th March?
3. What was the difference in temperature between the 1st and 3rd March?
4. How many hours of sunshine were there on the 6th March?

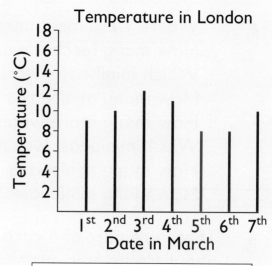

Temperature in London

Daily hours of sunshine						
1st	2nd	3rd	4th	5th	6th	7th
3	3	5	5	1	3	2

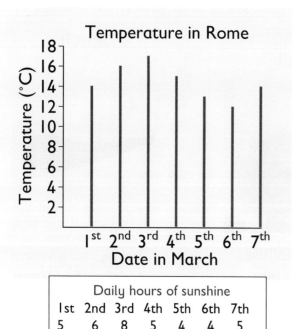

Temperature in Rome

Daily hours of sunshine						
1st	2nd	3rd	4th	5th	6th	7th
5	6	8	5	4	4	5

B Rome

1. What was the temperature in Rome on the 5th March?
2. Which day had the most hours of sunshine?
3. On which day did the temperature reach 17 °C?
4. What was the difference in temperature between the 4th and 6th March?

C Compare the temperature and hours of sunshine in London and Rome.

1. How much hotter was Rome on the 1st March?
2. On which day did they both have the same hours of sunshine?
3. How many more hours of sunshine did Rome have on the 3rd March?
4. On which day was Rome 6 °C hotter than London?

This is a ten day weather record kept by Class 4.

Date (March)	Name	Time	Temp.	Sky	Wind	Wind direction
Mon. 13th	Roger	10:30am	11°C	clear	breeze	East
Tues. 14th	Norman	10:35am	10°C	clear	breeze	North East
Wed. 15th	Emma	10:33am	11°C	grey	light breeze	North East
Thurs. 16th	Balvir	10:27am	11°C	grey	fresh wind	North
Fri. 17th	Wai	10:30am	12°C	cloudy	fresh wind	North
Mon. 20th	Sarah	10:32am	13°C	grey	windy	East
Tues. 21st	Raj	10:37am	12°C	cloudy	strong wind	North East
Wed. 22nd	Shoko	10:28am	14°C	cloudy	fresh wind	South East

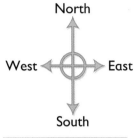

North

West ← → East

South

13th	
14th	
15th	
16th	
17th	
20th	
21st	
22nd	

	sunshine
	clear
	partly cloudy
	very cloudy
	rain

A Use the charts and diagrams to answer these questions.

1. Which day had the highest temperature?
2. Who recorded the weather on the 21st March?
3. In which direction did the wind mostly blow from?
4. On which two days did it rain?
5. Which was the windiest day?
6. On how many days did the wind blow from the North?
7. Why do you think the records were all taken at about the same time?

B 1. Draw a graph to show the temperatures recorded for these eight days.
2. Write about two things that the graph shows you.

Things to do!

■ Keep a weather record yourself.

■ Use charts and diagrams to show any patterns in the changing weather.

Longest bridges

George Washington (1931)
New York City, USA
Length: 1067 m

Golden Gate (1937)
San Francisco, USA
Length: 1280 m

Mackinac Straits (1957)
Michigan, USA
Length: 1158 m

Forth Road Bridge (1964)
Firth of Forth, Scotland
Length: 1006 m

Verrazano-Narrows (1964)
New York City, USA
Length: 1298 m

Severn (1966)
Severn Estuary, England
Length: 988 m

Tagus River Bridge (1966)
Lisbon, Portugal
Length: 1013 m

Bosporus (1973)
Istanbul, Turkey
Length: 1074 m

Humber Estuary (1980)
Humber, England
Length: 1410 m

Akashi–Kaikyo (to be
completed in 1997)
Honshu-shikoku, Japan
Length: 1780 m

A Copy and complete this graph.

Put the spans in order of length.

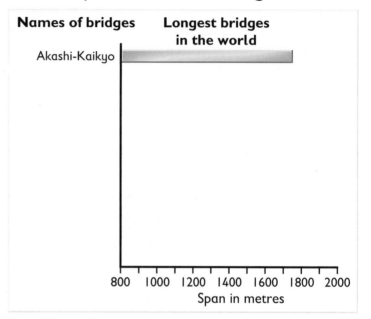

B
1. Which is the longest bridge in Britain?
2. How many metres long is the Golden Gate Bridge?
3. How much longer is the Forth Road Bridge than the Severn Bridge?
4. Which bridges were completed before 1960?
5. Which bridge is seven metres longer than the George Washington Bridge?
6. Which bridges are over 1200 m in length?

Data

Josh and Becky are trying to find out if the shape of their bridge makes a difference to its strength.

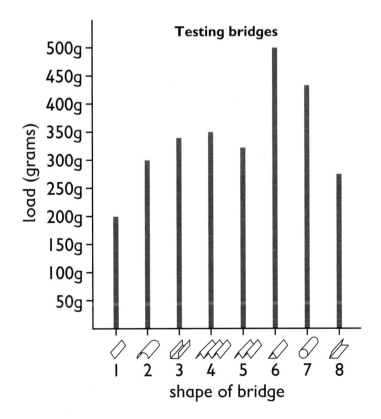

1. What load did 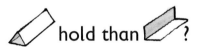 hold?

2. How much more did ✏ hold than ◣ ?

3. Which is the strongest shape?

4. Which shape carried a load of 430 g?

5. Which shape carried 50 g more than ◗ ?

Ashburn Swimming Pool

Each 🏊 represents 20 people.
🏊🏊 represents between 40 and 60 people.

	Number of visitors to Ashburn Swimming Pool
Sun	🏊🏊🏊🏊🏊🏊🏊🏊🏊
Mon	🏊🏊🏊🏊🏊
Tue	🏊🏊🏊🏊🏊
Wed	🏊🏊🏊🏊🏊🏊
Thurs	🏊🏊🏊
Fri	🏊🏊🏊
Sat	🏊🏊🏊🏊🏊🏊🏊🏊🏊🏊

1. How many people visited Ashburn swimming pool on Wednesday?
2. On which day did between 80 and 100 people visit?
3. On which days did fewer than 100 people visit?
4. How many more people visited on Saturday than Friday?
5. What was the total number of visitors at the weekend?

This is a timetable of a Saturday for Hannah and David.

Time		Time	
7.00 am	wake up	4.00 pm	bus home
7.30 am	wash	4.30 pm	tidy bedroom and play
8.00 am	breakfast	6.00 pm	tea
8.30 am	bus to shops	6.30 pm	washing up
9.00 am	shopping with mum	7.00 pm	watch television
12.15 pm	lunch	8.00 pm	wash
1.00 pm	swimming	8.30 pm	bed / read a book

A This graph shows how David feels on Saturday.

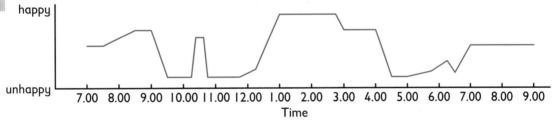

1. What does David most like doing?
2. What makes him unhappy?
3. What do you think happened at 10.30 am to make him happy?
4. Does David enjoy bus journeys?
5. What happened at 4.30 pm?

B

Hannah likes:
– reading books
– swimming
– going shopping
– playing

Hannah does not like:
– getting up in the morning
– going to bed
– washing up
– going on buses

Draw a similar graph for Hannah. Use the timetable of Hannah's Saturday to complete the graph.

Probability

A Decide whether these events are:

| impossible | likely | certain |

| very unlikely | unlikely | very likely |

1. I will be on a school bus tomorrow.

2. I will find a 50p coin this week.

3. It will get dark tonight.

4. The next time I roll a dice it will be 6.

5. Tomorrow will be Sunday.

6. I shall eat brown bread today.

B We use all sorts of words to describe the chance of something happening. Here are a few.

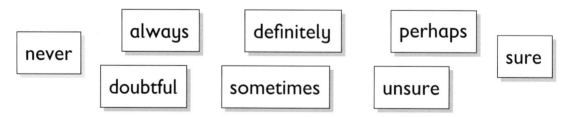

| never | always | definitely | perhaps | sure |

| doubtful | sometimes | unsure |

1. Write these chance words and add some more words of your own.
2. Use each of these in a sentence.
3. Put the words in some form of order.

Data

Even chance

A Daniel and Lucy are playing  'Pick a colour'

> If yellow is picked Daniel wins.
> If blue is picked Lucy wins.

1. Who has more chance of winning? Explain your answer.

2. Who has more chance of winning now?

3. How would you give Daniel and Lucy an even chance of winning?

B For each bag, write the chance of picking a red bead.

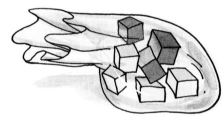

Less than even chance   Even chance   More than even chance

1.   2.   3.   4.

C What is the chance of spinning these colours on the spinners?

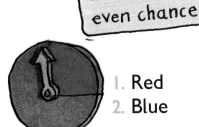

Less than even chance   Even chance   More than even chance

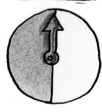

1. Red
2. Blue

3. Green
4. Yellow

5. Red
6. Green

Glossary

Adjacent	next door to each other. (5, 6, 7, 8 are adjacent numbers).
Angle	an amount of turn.
Arrow head	a 4-sided shape with two pairs of equal adjacent sides. One pair bend into the shape.
Cone	a 3D shape with a circle base from which a curved surface comes to a point.
Co-ordinates	a pair of numbers which describes the position of something.
Cube	a 3D shape which has six square faces.
Cuboid	a 3D shape which has either six rectangle faces, or four rectangle faces and two square faces.
Cylinder	a 3D shape with identical circle ends and a curved surface joining the circles together.
Degrees	used to measure angles. There are 90 degrees in one right angle.
Equilateral triangle	a triangle with three equal sides.
Hexagon	any 2D shape which has six straight sides.

Isosceles triangle	a triangle with two equal sides.	
Kite	a 4-sided shape with two pairs of equal adjacent sides.	
Net	an opened out 3D shape.	net of a cube
Oval	a flattened circle.	this oval is called an ellipse this oval is like an egg
Parallel lines	lines which keep the same distance apart.	
Parallelogram	a 4-sided shape with both pairs of opposite sides parallel.	rectangles, squares and rhombus are special parallelograms
Pentagon	any 2D shape with five straight sides.	
Polygon	any 2D shape with straight sides.	
Prism	a 3D shape with identical polygon ends and rectangles joining them.	
Protractor	used for measuring angles in degrees.	40°
Pyramid	a 3D shape with a polygon base and triangle faces meeting at a vertex.	

Glossary

Quadrilateral	any 4-sided shape with straight sides.
Rectangle	a 4-sided shape with four right angles and opposite sides the same length.

a square is a special rectangle

Rhombus	a parallelogram with sides the same length. Sometimes a rhombus is called a diamond.
Right angle triangle	a triangle containing a right angle.
Semi-circle	half a circle.
Scalene triangle	a triangle with all sides a different length.
Sphere	a 3D shape which is a perfectly round ball.
Square	a 4-sided shape with four right angles and four sides the same length.
Trapezium	a 4-sided shape with one pair of parallel sides.
Triangle	any 2D shape with three straight sides.
Triangle prism	a 3D shape with identical triangle ends and rectangles joining them together.
Vertex	the corner of a 3D shape. More than one vertex are called vertices.

vertex